606

THE DETROIT PISTONS

BY

MARK STEWART

Content Consultant
Matt Zeysing
Historian and Archivist
The Naismith Memorial Basketball Hall of Fame

NORWOOD HOUSE PRESS

CHICAGO, ILLINOIS

Norwood House Press
P.O. Box 316598
Chicago, Illinois 60631

For information regarding Norwood House Press, please visit our website at:
www.norwoodhousepress.com or call 866-565-2900.

All photos courtesy of AP/Wide World Photos, Inc. except the following:
Getty Images/Brian Bahr (cover): Capital Cards: (7 & 21 top); Bowman Gum, Inc. (14 left, 17 & 30);
Union Oil Company of California (20); Topps, Inc. (21 bottom, 39 bottom & 40);
TCMA (36). Special thanks to Capital Cards and Topps, Inc.

Editor: Mike Kennedy
Designer: Ron Jaffe
Project Management: Black Book Partners, LLC.

Special thanks to Kathleen Baxter.

Library of Congress Cataloging-in-Publication Data

Stewart, Mark, 1960–
    The Detroit Pistons / by Mark Stewart ; content consultant, Matt Zeysing.
        p. cm. -- (Team spirit)
    Summary: "Presents the history, accomplishments and key personalities of
the Detroit Pistons basketball team. Includes timelines, quotes, maps,
glossary and websites"--Provided by publisher.
    Includes bibliographical references and index.
    ISBN-13: 978-1-59953-008-6 (library edition : alk. paper)
    ISBN-10: 1-59953-008-2 (library edition : alk. paper)
    1. Detroit Pistons (Basketball team)--History--Juvenile literature. I.
Zeysing, Matt. II. Title. III. Series.
    GV885.52.D47S84 2006
                                                            2005033674

Manufactured in the United States of America.

COVER PHOTO: The Pistons celebrate a win during the 2005 playoffs.

Table of Contents

CHAPTER	PAGE
Meet the Pistons	4
Way Back When	6
The Team Today	10
Home Court	12
Dressed For Success	14
We Won!	16
Go-To Guys	20
On the Sidelines	24
One Great Day	26
Legend Has It	28
It Really Happened	30
Team Spirit	32
Timeline	34
Fun Facts	36
Talking Hoops	38
For the Record	40
Pinpoints	42
Play Ball	44
Glossary	46
Places to Go	47
Index	48

SPORTS WORDS & VOCABULARY WORDS: In this book, you will find many words that are new to you. You may also see familiar words used in new ways. The glossary on page 46 gives the meanings of basketball words, as well as "everyday" words that have special basketball meanings. These words appear in **bold type** throughout the book. The glossary on page 47 gives the meanings of vocabulary words that are not related to basketball. They appear in ***bold italic type*** throughout the book.

BASKETBALL SEASONS: Because each basketball season begins late in one year and ends early in the next, seasons are not named after years. Instead, they are written out as two years separated by a dash, for example 1944–45 or 2005–06.

Meet the Pistons

Tough, talented, brave enough to be different—if you are a member of the Detroit Pistons, these are the rules you live by. Every season, the team finds new and interesting ways to combine the skills of its players. The names on the uniforms may change, but never the spirit of the team. The Pistons have been dribbling the ball to their own beat for more than 60 years!

Like the city they play for, the Pistons never stop trying. Their fans feel like part of the team, and the players feel the same way. Whether the Pistons are winning championships, or starting over with new stars, they make basketball fun.

This book explores the great moments, great players, and great teams that have made the Pistons one of basketball's most successful and interesting teams. A special kind of team spirit is only part of the picture. By looking at the Pistons from many different angles, you will begin to see the players, coaches and fans in a whole new way.

The Pistons players have a special bond with one another.
This closeness helped them win the NBA Championship in 2004.

Way Back When

I n the early days of basketball, the best players did not always play for **professional** teams. There was not much money to be made in the sport back then. After a college star *graduated*, he would use his education to find a good job. He would work during the

day, and play basketball for his company's team on evenings and weekends. As you might imagine, a company that hired a lot of college stars would have a very good team. The competition between company teams soon became very fierce.

During the 1930s, a factory owner named Fred Zollner decided to make his basketball team the best in the United States. His company manufactured pistons, which are the metal *cylinders* that pump back

Fred Zollner talks business with his sister, a part-owner of Zollner Enterprises.

6

Bobby McDermott, a player and coach for the Pistons during the 1940s.

and forth in a motor. Zollner personally scouted and signed some of the top players in the sport. They worked for the Zollner Machine Works during the day. At night, these men would trade their shirts and ties for uniforms and become the Pistons.

In 1941, the Pistons were invited to join the **National Basketball League (NBL)**, one of the first big professional leagues. Zollner agreed, and by the end of their third season, the Pistons were NBL champions. In 1944, their two big stars—Bobby McDermott and Buddy Jeannette—helped them win the World Professional Basketball Tournament. In 1947, the Pistons joined the Basketball Association of America, which would become the **National Basketball Association (NBA)**.

During the 1940s and early 1950s, the Pistons did not play in Detroit, as they do today. The Zollner factory was located in Fort Wayne, Indiana, so they were known as the Ft. Wayne Pistons.

During the 1950s, the Ft. Wayne Pistons were one of the most exciting teams in the NBA. They reached the **NBA Finals** twice in the *decade*, but fell short of a championship both times. In 1955, they lost Game Seven by a single point. Their best player during this time was high-scoring George Yardley.

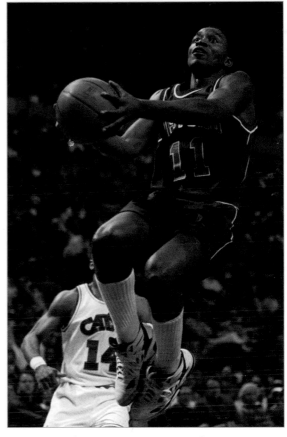

The Pistons moved to Detroit in 1957, when Zollner moved his piston *plant* to Michigan. They did not reach the NBA Finals again for more than 30 years. Some very good players wore the Detroit uniform during this time, including Bailey Howell, Dave DeBusschere, Dave Bing, and Bob Lanier. All four are now in the **Hall of Fame**.

The Pistons finally won their first NBA championship in 1989. A year later, they won again. The Pistons of 1989 and 1990 were led by Isiah Thomas and nicknamed the "Bad Boys," because they played a rough style of basketball. Other teams hated to face Detroit, but as always, Detroit fans loved their Pistons.

LEFT: George Yardley, the first pro to score 2,000 points in a season.
TOP: Isiah Thomas, the leader of the 1989 and 1990 NBA champions.

The Team Today

Playing for the Pistons means you are a part of basketball history. When today's players look up and see all of the banners and **retired jerseys** hanging from the *rafters*, they are reminded of the team's long *tradition*. When they look at each other, they know that it takes a true team effort to win.

The Pistons have always had good players, but it is only when they pull together that they *contend* for championships. In 2004 and 2005, Detroit reached the NBA Finals without a single "superstar." They succeeded by sharing the basketball, and by playing good team defense.

The Pistons arc an exciting team to watch. Any player is likely to get "hot" at any time, and when he does, his teammates will keep **feeding** him the basketball. When other teams prepare to play the Pistons, they never know who will *emerge* as Detroit's hero.

There is one thing opponents can always count on when they face the Pistons. The team that takes the floor will play with a lot of determination, and a lot of attitude.

Ben Wallace, Darvin Ham, and Chauncey Billups
watch from the bench as a teammate puts up a shot.

Home Court

The Pistons play in the Palace of Auburn Hills. It is a beautiful basketball arena located just outside the city of Detroit. The Palace is one of the NBA's best arenas. All of the seats offer good views, and they are comfortable, too.

The team moved into the arena at the beginning of the 1988–89 season. The following spring, the Pistons were crowned NBA champions. They claimed the championship again in 1990. **Winning it all** in each of the Palace's first two seasons has given the building a special feel. Opponents know they are in for a battle whenever they visit there.

THE PALACE BY THE NUMBERS

- *There are 22,076 seats in the Palace of Auburn Hills.*
- *Seven retired jersey numbers hang from the Palace ceiling: Chuck Daly (2), Joe Dumars (4), Isiah Thomas (11), Vinnie Johnson (15), Bob Lanier (16), Dave Bing (21), and Bill Laimbeer (40).*
- *In the arena's first game, on November 5, 1988, the Pistons defeated the Charlotte Hornets 94–85.*
- *The first playoff game at the Palace was a 101–91 win against the Boston Celtics on April 28, 1989.*

The Palace of Auburn Hills goes wild as the Pistons win the 2004 NBA title.

Dressed for Success

The Pistons' uniforms have changed a lot since the 1940s. In the early years, the team's jersey advertised the Zollner Pistons. Later, the Zollner name was replaced by the team's home cities, first Ft. Wayne and then Detroit. The team has almost always had a color combination of red, white and blue.

During the 1990s, the Pistons used a horse logo on a uniform that was greenish-blue. This was not a popular style. When the team returned to its basic red-white-and-blue uniform, the fans were very happy.

ABOVE: Ralph Hamilton sports an old Zollner Pistons jersey.
RIGHT: Grant Hill wears the "horse-head" uniform during a 1999 game.

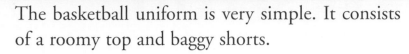

UNIFORM BASICS

The basketball uniform is very simple. It consists of a roomy top and baggy shorts.

- The top hangs from the shoulders, with big "scoops" for the arms and neck. This style has not changed much over the years.

- Shorts, however, have changed a lot. They used to be very short, so players could move their legs freely. In the last 20 years, shorts have actually gotten longer and much baggier.

Basketball uniforms look the same as they did long ago...until you look very closely. In the old days, the shorts had belts and buckles. The tops were made of a thick cotton called "jersey," which got very heavy when players sweated. Later, uniforms were made of shiny *satin*. They may have looked great, but they did not "breathe." Players got very hot! Today, most uniforms are made of *synthetic* materials that soak up sweat and keep the body cool.

Richard Hamilton models a recent Pistons uniform. He is also wearing a mask to protect an injury.

We Won!

During the 1940s, basketball's best teams were crowned at the World Professional Basketball Tournament, in Chicago, Illinois. This event brought together teams from professional leagues, "touring" teams (like the Harlem Globetrotters), and teams that were sponsored by companies, like Fred Zollner's Pistons. The Pistons won this tournament three years in a row. They beat the Brooklyn Eagles 50–33 in 1944, the Dayton Acmes 78–52 in 1945, and the Oshkosh All-Stars 73–57 in 1946.

The star of the Pistons during these championship years was Bobby McDermott. McDermott was a guard who used a two-handed set shot to score from anywhere within 35 feet of the basket. He was **player-coach** of the Pistons during their 1944 championship,

Bobby McDermott

Ed Sadowski

and scored 14 points in the finals against the Eagles. McDermott scored 15 in the 1945 title game, and 20 in the 1946 championship. Other stars on these Pistons teams included Buddy Jeannette, Jake Pelkington, and Ed Sadowski.

The Pistons waited more than 40 years before they returned to the winner's circle. During the 1980s, coach Chuck Daly built a tough and talented team around guards Isiah Thomas and Joe Dumars, and center Bill Laimbeer. Just as important were the Pistons' **role players**. Dennis Rodman was a great rebounder and defender, Mark Aguirre was a bruising **power forward**, and guard Vinnie Johnson was a valuable "**sixth man**."

The Pistons faced the Los Angeles Lakers in the 1989 NBA Finals. The Lakers had beaten them in the finals the year before, but this time the Pistons could not be stopped. They swept Magic Johnson and Kareem Abdul-Jabbar right off the court, four games to none. Detroit returned to the NBA Finals for the third time in a row in 1990. Their opponent, the Portland Trail Blazers, won just one game. The Pistons were champions again.

In 2004, the Pistons took the NBA title again. They defeated the Lakers in the finals. It was a very special victory, because the experts believed a team could not win it all without at least one superstar player. The Pistons proved them wrong. The starting five of Chauncey Billups, Richard Hamilton, Tayshaun Prince, Rasheed Wallace, and Ben Wallace may not have sounded like an **All-Star squad**, but they were good enough to defeat Kobe Bryant and Shaquille O'Neal in five games.

TOP: The Pistons celebrate their 1989 NBA championship.
RIGHT: Chauncey Billups, the MVP of the 2004 NBA Finals.

Go-To Guys

To be a true star in the NBA, you need more than a great shot. You have to be a "go-to guy"—someone teammates trust to make the winning play when the seconds are ticking away in a big game. Detroit fans have had a lot to cheer about over the years, including these great stars…

THE PIONEERS

BOBBY McDERMOTT   5' 11" Guard

• BORN: 1/7/1914   • DIED: 10/3/1963   • PLAYED FOR TEAM: 1941–42 TO 1945–46

Bobby McDermott was the last of the great "set-shot" artists. With both feet planted on the floor, he would toss the ball high in the air with two hands, releasing his shot at eye level. McDermott was basketball's **Most Valuable Player (MVP)** five years in a row during the 1940s.

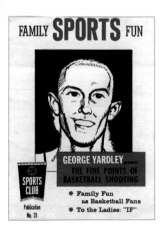

GEORGE YARDLEY   6' 5" Forward

• BORN: 11/3/1928   • DIED: 8/12/2004

• PLAYED FOR TEAM: 1953–54 TO 1958–59

George Yardley was one of the players who pioneered the jumpshot. He was also the first player to score more than 2,000 points in a season. Yardley led the Pistons to the NBA Finals in 1955 and 1956.

DAVE DeBUSSCHERE   6' 6" Forward

- BORN: 10/16/1940   • DIED: 5/14/2003
- PLAYED FOR TEAM: 1962–63 TO 1968–69

Dave DeBusschere was more than a great all-around player. He was also a great leader. In 1964, the Pistons made DeBusschere the NBA's youngest coach. He was only 24 years old.

DAVE BING   6' 3" Guard

- BORN: 11/24/1943   • PLAYED FOR TEAM: 1966–67 TO 1974–75

Dave Bing was one of the NBA's "nice guys." An accident when he was a child left him with blurry vision in one eye. Bing was good enough to overcome this disability and lead the NBA in scoring 1968.

BOB LANIER   6'11" Center

BOB LANIER • C

- BORN: 9/10/1948
- PLAYED FOR TEAM: 1970–71 TO 1979–80

Bob Lanier was one of the best shooters and rebounders to ever play in the NBA. He moved his enormous body with the quickness and grace of a much smaller player. Lanier represented Detroit in the All-Star Game seven times.

LEFT: George Yardley
TOP: Dave DeBusschere   **RIGHT**: Bob Lanier

ISIAH THOMAS   6' 1" Guard

• BORN: 4/30/1961   • PLAYED FOR TEAM: 1981–82 TO 1993–94

Isiah Thomas was the most exciting star in Pistons history. When he was hot, no one in basketball could stop him. He was a fearless player who loved to challenge opponents. Thomas led the Pistons to their first two NBA championships.

JOE DUMARS   6' 3" Guard

• BORN: 5/24/1963

• PLAYED FOR TEAM: 1985–86 TO 1998–99

Joe Dumars was one of the best defensive players in NBA history. He was often the man chosen to guard the other team's best shooter. The Pistons could also count on him whenever they needed a **clutch basket**. Dumars was a winner as a player, and later became the team's president.

DENNIS RODMAN   6' 8" Forward

• BORN: 5/13/1961   • PLAYED FOR TEAM: 1986–87 TO 1992–93

Dennis Rodman seemed to know where a missed shot would bounce before it even hit the rim. This made him one of the best rebounders in NBA history. Rodman was also one of the league's finest defensive players.

GRANT HILL   6' 8" Forward

- BORN: 10/5/1972 • PLAYED FOR TEAM: 1994–95 TO 1999–2000

Grant Hill had as much ability as anyone who has ever worn a Detroit uniform. He was voted All-NBA in each of his first six seasons in the league—all with the Pistons.

BEN WALLACE   6' 9" Forward

- BORN: 9/10/1974 • FIRST SEASON WITH TEAM: 2000–01

Ben Wallace was a **bench-warmer** before he joined the Pistons in 2000. With Detroit, he made himself into the NBA's best rebounder and most feared defensive player.

RICHARD HAMILTON   6' 6" Guard/Forward

- BORN: 2/14/1978 • FIRST SEASON WITH TEAM: 2002–03

Richard Hamilton already was a good shooter when the Pistons traded for him in 2002. He proved he was a great winner when he helped the team reach the NBA Finals in 2004 and 2005.

RASHEED WALLACE

6' 11" Center

- BORN: 9/17/1974 • FIRST SEASON WITH TEAM: 2003–04

Rasheed Wallace gave the Pistons the tough, high-scoring big man they needed to win the championship.

LEFT: Joe Dumars **RIGHT**: Ben Wallace (left) and Rasheed Wallace fight Tim Duncan for a rebound.

On the Sidelines

Fred Zollner, the man who started the Pistons, never earned much money from basketball. His company was another story. The pistons he sold to car-makers made him very rich. In 1957, Zollner moved his factory from Ft. Wayne to Detroit so he could be closer to his customers—and the Pistons went with him.

The Pistons have had many coaches since then. For a long time, their most famous coach was Charley Eckman. Eckman was an NBA referee before Zollner hired him. This was the first—and last—time a referee ever coached an NBA team.

The two best coaches in team history were Chuck Daly and Larry Brown. Both men taught the Pistons to share the ball and play good defense.

Daly had a winning record in all nine seasons that he coached the Pistons, and won two championships. Brown led the Pistons to the 2004 NBA championship in his first year as the team's coach.

Larry Brown congratulates his players after winning the NBA title in 2004. He coached in the league for 21 years before winning his first championship.

One Great Day

When the 2004 NBA Finals began, no one outside Detroit believed the Pistons had a chance to beat the Los Angeles Lakers. The Pistons had good players and a smart coach, but the Lakers had four future Hall of Famers (Shaquille O'Neal, Kobe Bryant, Karl Malone, and Gary Payton) in their lineup—and their coach, Phil Jackson, had won 10 championship rings (nine as a coach and one as a player).

Coach Larry Brown gave the Pistons a plan that depended on teamwork and timing. He promised them that if they played basketball "the right way," they had a chance to win. The Pistons did a good job defending against the Lakers' offense, and forced Bryant and O'Neal to take difficult shots. For the Pistons, there was a new hero every night. The Lakers did not know who to **double-team** from one game to the next. The Pistons won three of the first four games, and needed just one more victory for the championship.

Ben Wallace and Chauncey Billups go for the high five. They were the stars of Game Five for the Pistons.

Game Five was played in the Palace of Auburn Hills. The noise was *deafening* as the teams took the floor. On this night, the Lakers were in deep trouble. Every Detroit starter scored 10 or more points, including Ben Wallace, who was known more for his defense and rebounding. "Big Ben" poured in 18 points and grabbed 22 rebounds. More important, he was fouled so many times by O'Neal that the Lakers had to sit their All-Star center on the bench.

The Pistons took control of the game in the the third quarter. They outscored the Lakers 27–14 to build an 82–59 lead. When the final buzzer sounded, the Pistons had won, 100–87. Chauncey Billups was named the MVP, but anyone on the team could have won the award. It was a great day for Detroit, and a great day for basketball.

27

Legend Has It

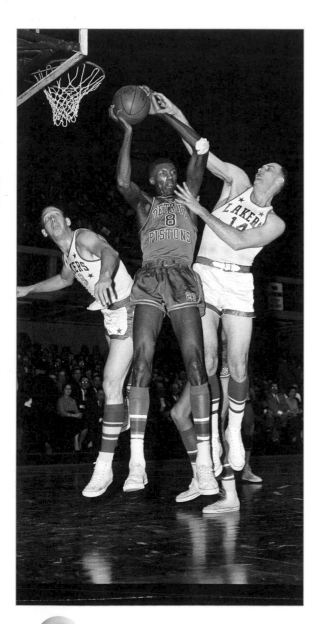

Why did Walter Dukes wear a cow bell in practice?

LEGEND HAS IT that his teammates wanted to hear him coming. Dukes was known for swinging his long arms without looking. During games, the referees **whistled** him for many fouls. In practice, he hit his own teammates so often they they demanded that the coach do something about it. The Pistons made Dukes wear a cow bell, and his teammates got slugged less often.

Walter Dukes grabs a rebound against the Minneapolis Lakers in a 1959 game. Note the bandage on his left elbow.

Why did the Pistons trade George Yardley the season after he scored more than 2,000 points?

LEGEND HAS IT that Fred Zollner's girlfriend did not think a team's best player should be bald. She talked the Pistons' owner into benching Yardley (right) during the 1958–59 season, even though he had set a record with 2,001 points the year before. Later, after he broke his hand in a game, he was traded to the Syracuse Nationals.

Did destiny bring Chauncey Billups to the Pistons?

LEGEND HAS IT that it did. When Billups was a teenager, his favorite player was Joe Dumars of the Pistons, who was MVP of the 1989 NBA Finals. During the summer of 2002, after Billups had been **cut** by the Minnesota Timberwolves, Dumars called him. Billups could not believe his ears. Dumars was now Detroit's team president. He said Billups was the "missing piece" to the Pistons' championship puzzle, and signed him to a contract. In 2004, Billups led Detroit to the title and was named MVP of the NBA Finals, just like his hero Dumars.

It Really Happened

If you watch a lot of NBA basketball, you have probably noticed a little red clock that counts down from 24 every time a team gets the ball. This is the 24-second shot clock. If a team fails to try a shot before it reaches zero, it loses the ball

When the NBA began, there *was* no shot clock. This started to change in 1950, thanks in part to the Pistons. In a game against the Minneapolis Lakers, the Pistons held the ball as long as they could every time they came down the court. Why? Because they had no

one to guard the Lakers' great center, George Mikan. The Lakers would pass the ball to Mikan near the basket, and he was too big and strong to stop. Murray Mendenhall, Detroit's coach, decided that the longer the ball was in the hands of the Pistons, the less time it would be in Mikan's hands—and the fewer points he would be able to score. The **strategy** worked. The Pistons won 19–18!

There was just one problem—the fans did not enjoy the game. They booed all night long. They had paid a lot of money to watch the Pistons and Lakers, and they felt cheated by the boring style of play.

The NBA worried that these fans would never come back. In 1954, the league began using the 24-second clock. It kept teams from stalling—and did a whole lot more. The shot clock created a new type of player who "attacked" the basket. This led to the kind of exciting basketball you see today.

LEFT: Curly Armstrong, one of the players who stalled against the Lakers.
ABOVE: George Mikan, the biggest (and best) player in the early days of the NBA, is fitted for a suit.

800-333-ROCK
rockfinancial.com
The DEFENDERS
PISTONS
800-333-ROCK
800-333-ROCK
Rock Financial PRESENTS
WE BELIEV
PISTONS
23

Team Spirit

Pistons fans are famous for supporting their team. They are very loud and very proud. They will dress in wild costumes and paint themselves in team colors. Over the years, there have been several famous fans. One man was called Joe the "Brow" for his bushy eyebrows. He ran around the arena leading cheers and *taunting* the visiting players. Another was Dancing Ernie, who did weird dances in the upper sections of the Palace.

For many years, Detroit had the NBA's highest attendance. The Pistons once sold out 245 games in a row. During the 1987–88 season, when the team reached the NBA Finals, more than one million fans bought tickets to their games.

Detroit fans know the personalities of their players. They can sense when the Pistons need some extra energy, and they know how to provide it. They also know how to distract visiting players. This makes the Pistons very hard to beat on their home court.

Pistons fans are known for their energy and excitement.

Timeline

The basketball season is played from October through June. That means each season takes place at the end of one year and the beginning of the next. In this timeline, the accomplishments of the Pistons are shown by season.

1943–44
The Pistons defeat the Sheboygan Redskins to win the NBL championship.

1957–58
The team moves from Ft. Wayne to Detroit.

1954–55
Coach Charley Eckman leads the Pistons to the NBA Finals.

1964–65
The Pistons make 24-year-old Dave DeBusschere their player-coach.

Charley Eckman

Dave DeBusschere

Chuck
Daly

Grant
Hill

1988–89
Chuck Daly coaches the Pistons
to their first NBA championship.

1994–95
Grant Hill is voted
Co-Rookie of the Year.

1967–68
Dave Bing becomes the
first guard since 1948
to win the scoring title.

1989–90
The Pistons win the
championship for the
second year in a row.

2003–04
The Pistons beat the Los
Angeles Lakers for their
third NBA championship.

All eyes are on
Larry Brown as
he calls a play
during the
2004 NBA
Finals.

Fun Facts

NOTHING BUT AIR

Thanks to their wealthy owner, the Pistons traveled in style in the 1950s. The team used the Zollner company plane to go from game to game. Other NBA teams had to take the train.

Dave DeBusschere

MY OTHER JOB

Dave DeBusschere—a player and coach for the Pistons in the 1960s—was also a pitcher for the Chicago White Sox. Dick Groat, a Piston in 1952–53, was an All-Star shortstop for the Pittsburgh Pirates.

BIG FOOT

Bob Lanier wore size 22 basketball shoes. They had to be specially made for the 6' 11" center.

THIS PLACE IS HUGE!

During the 1980s, the Pistons played their home games in the Pontiac Silverdome, a gigantic football stadium.

NO PAIN, NO GAIN

In Game Six of the 1988 NBA Finals, Isiah Thomas set a record by scoring 25 points in the third quarter against the Los Angeles Lakers. Fourteen of those points came after he had sprained his ankle!

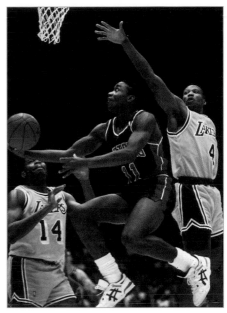
Isiah Thomas

JUST PUSH "START"

Vinnie Johnson was nicknamed the "Microwave." He could come into the game and get hot within seconds.

MANE MAN

There was no such thing as a bad hair day for Ben Wallace. He had the league's "baddest" hair *every* day!

Ben Wallace

Talking Hoops

Richard Hamilton

"The fans here made me feel right at home. They're very loyal. Even when we didn't win a lot of games, they were very supportive."

—*Grant Hill, on the Detroit fans*

"I'd much rather be a **second fiddle** on a contender than a so-called 'superstar' on a bad team."

—*Richard Hamilton, on playing as part of a team*

"Most guys had **vertical leaps** of about a foot. I had thirty-two inches, which would make me an average jumper today. But that was the best in the NBA at that time."

—*George Yardley, on basketball in the 1950s*

"This particular collection of individuals was the reason we won the world championship. No individual was greater than the team."

—*Isiah Thomas, on the 1988-89 Pistons*

Isiah Thomas

"I love being *in the trenches*, doing the 'dirty work,' mixing it up."

—*Ben Wallace, on playing defense and rebounding*

Dave Bing

"Your man can't score and can't shoot if he doesn't have the ball, so that's a first rule of defense no matter what position you play—keep your man from getting the ball."

—*Dave Bing, on playing defense*

For the Record

T he great Pistons teams and players have left their marks on the record books. These are the "best of the best"…

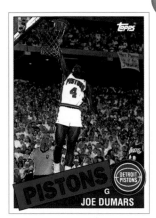

Joe Dumars

Grant Hill

PISTONS AWARD WINNERS

WINNER	AWARD	SEASON
Don Meineke	Rookie of the Year*	1952–53
Dave Bing	Rookie of the Year	1966–67
Bob Lanier	All-Star Game MVP	1973–74
Ray Scott	Coach of the Year	1973–74
Isiah Thomas	All-Star Game MVP	1983–84
Isiah Thomas	All-Star Game MVP	1985–86
Joe Dumars	Finals MVP	1988–89
Isiah Thomas	Finals MVP	1989–90
Dennis Rodman	Defensive Player of the Year	1989–90
Dennis Rodman	Defensive Player of the Year	1990–91
Grant Hill	Co-Rookie of the Year	1994–95
Rick Carlisle	Coach of the Year	2001–02
Ben Wallace	Defensive Player of the Year	2001–02
Ben Wallace	Defensive Player of the Year	2002–03
Ben Wallace	Defensive Player of the Year	2004–05
Chauncey Billups	Finals MVP	2003–04

The Rookie of the Year award is given to the league's best first-year player.

PISTONS ACHIEVEMENTS

ACHIEVEMENT	SEASON
1944 World Pro Champions	1943–44
NBL Champions	1943–44
1945 World Pro Champions	1944–45
NBL Champions	1944–45
1946 World Pro Champions	1945–46
NBA Champions	1988–89
NBA Champions	1989–90
NBA Champions	2003–04

ABOVE: Rookie of the Year Dave Bing looks for an open teammate. **LEFT**: Vinnie Johnson, James Edwards, and John Salley—the bench players that helped the Pistons win it all in 1989 and 1990.

Pinpoints

T he history of a basketball team is made up of many smaller stories. These stories take place all over the map—not just in the city a team calls "home." Match the push-pins on these maps to the Team Facts and you will begin to see the story of the Pistons unfold!

TEAM FACTS

1. Fort Wayne, Indiana—*The Pistons began here.*
2. Detroit, Michigan—*The Pistons have played in this area since 1957.*
3. Buffalo, New York—*Bob Lanier was born here.*
4. Chicago, Illinois—*Isiah Thomas was born here.*
5. Portland, Oregon—*The Pistons won their second. NBA championship here, in 1990.*
6. Hollywood, California—*George Yardley was born here.*
7. Denver, Colorado—*Chauncey Billups was born here.*
8. Shreveport, Louisiana—*Joe Dumars was born here.*
9. Washington, D.C.—*Dave Bing was born here.*
10. Trenton, New Jersey—*Dennis Rodman was born here.*
11. Queens, New York—*Bobby McDermott was born here.*
12. Novi Sad, Montenegro—*Darko Milicic was born here.*

Darko Milicic, the team's top pick in the 2003 draft.

Play Ball

Basketball is a sport played by two teams of five players. NBA games have four 12-minute quarters—48 minutes in all—and the team that scores the most points when time has run out is the winner. Most baskets count for two points. Players who make shots from beyond the three-point line receive an extra point. Baskets made from the free-throw line count for one point. Free throws are penalty shots awarded to a team, usually after an opponent has committed a foul. A foul is called when one player makes hard contact with another.

Players can move around all they want, but the player with the ball cannot. He must bounce the ball with one hand or the other (but never both) in order to go from one part of the court to another. As long as he keeps "dribbling," he can keep moving.

In the NBA, teams must attempt a shot every 24 seconds, so there is little time to waste. The job of the defense is to make it as difficult as possible to take a good shot—and to grab the ball if the other team shoots and misses.

This may sound simple, but anyone who has played the game knows that basketball can be very complicated. Every player on the court has a job to do. Different players have different strengths and weaknesses. The coach must mix these players in just the right way, and teach them to work together as one.

The more you play and watch basketball, the more "little things" you are likely to notice. The next time you are at a game, look for these plays:

PLAY LIST

ALLEY-OOP—A play where the passer throws the ball just to the side of the rim—so a teammate can catch it and dunk in one motion.

BACK-DOOR PLAY—A play where the passer waits for his teammate to fake the defender away from the basket—then throws him the ball when he cuts back toward the basket.

KICK-OUT—A play where the ball-handler waits for the defense to surround him—then quickly passes to a teammate who is open for an outside shot. The ball is not really kicked in this play; the term comes from the action of pinball machines.

NO-LOOK PASS—A play where the passer fools a defender (with his eyes) into covering one teammate—then suddenly passes to another without looking.

PICK-AND-ROLL—A play where one teammate blocks or "picks off" another's defender with his body—then cuts to the basket for a pass in the confusion.

Glossary

BASKETBALL WORDS TO KNOW

ALL-STAR SQUAD—A team made up of the league's best players.

BENCH-WARMER—A player who spends most of the game sitting out, where he "warms the bench."

CLUTCH BASKET—A shot made under pressure.

CUT—Taken off a team.

DOUBLE-TEAM—Guard an opponent with two defenders.

FEEDING—Passing the ball to a teammate.

HALL OF FAME—The place where the game's greatest players are honored; these players are often called "Hall of Famers."

MOST VALUABLE PLAYER (MVP)—An award given each year to the league's best player; also given to the top player in the league finals and All-Star Game.

NATIONAL BASKETBALL ASSOCIATION (NBA)—The professional league that has been operating since the 1946–47 season.

NATIONAL BASKETBALL LEAGUE (NBL)—An early professional league that played 12 seasons, from 1937–38 to 1948–49.

NBA FINALS—The playoff series which decides the championship of the league.

PLAYER-COACH—An individual who performs as both player and coach at the same time.

POWER FORWARD—A forward who is big enough to play close to the basket; a team's other forward is often called a "small forward."

PROFESSIONAL—A person or team that plays a sport for money. College players are not paid, so they are considered "amateurs."

RETIRED JERSEYS—Uniform numbers of great players that cannot be worn again.

ROLE PLAYERS—People who are asked to do specific things when they are in a game.

SIXTH MAN—The first substitute to come into a game.

VERTICAL LEAP—A measure of how high a player can jump off the ground.

WHISTLED—Called for a violation by the referee.

WINNING IT ALL—Winning the championship.

OTHER WORDS TO KNOW

CONTEND—Compete for a prize or championship.

CYLINDERS—Parts of an engine.

DEAFENING—So loud that it affects the ability to hear.

DECADE—A period of 10 years.

GRADUATED—Received a diploma.

EMERGE—Come out of.

IN THE TRENCHES—A military term meaning on the front lines, where hand-to-hand combat takes place.

PLANT—Factory and offices.

RAFTERS—The supports that hold up a roof.

SATIN—A smooth, shiny fabric.

SECOND FIDDLE—A supporting role that is not always noticed.

STRATEGY—A plan or method for succeeding.

SYNTHETIC—Made in a laboratory, not in nature.

TRADITION—A belief or custom that is handed down from generation to generation.

TAUNTING—Teasing or challenging.

Places to Go

ON THE ROAD

THE PALACE OF AUBURN HILLS
Four Championship Drive
Auburn Hills, MI 48326
(248) 377-0100

NAISMITH MEMORIAL BASKETBALL HALL OF FAME
1000 West Columbus Avenue
Springfield, MA 01105
(877) 4HOOPLA

ON THE WEB

THE NATIONAL BASKETBALL ASSOCIATION   www.nba.com
  • *to learn more about the league's teams, players, and history*

THE DETROIT PISTONS   www.Pistons.com
  • *to learn more about the Detroit Pistons*

THE BASKETBALL HALL OF FAME   www.hoophall.com
  • *to learn more about history's greatest players*

ON THE BOOKSHELF

To learn more about the sport of basketball, look for these books at your library or bookstore:

  • Burgan, Michael. *Great Moments in Basketball.* New York, NY.: World Almanac, 2002.
  • Ingram, Scott. *A Basketball All-Star.* Chicago, IL.: Heinemann Library, 2005.
  • Suen, Anastasia. *The Story of Basketball.* New York, NY.: PowerKids Press, 2002.

Index

PAGE NUMBERS IN **BOLD** REFER TO ILLUSTRATIONS.

Abdul-Jabbar, Kareem............17
Aguirre, Mark.......................17
Armstrong, Curly **30**
Basketball Association
of America (BAA)...................7
Billups, Chauncey............**10**, 18,
 19, 27, **27**, 29, 40, 43
Bing, Dave 9, 13, 21, 35,
 39, **39**, 40, **41**, 43
Brown, Larry **24**, 25,
 26, 35, **35**
Bryant, Kobe...................18, 26
Carlisle, Rick......................40
Daly, Chuck.....13, 17, 25, 35, **35**
Dancing Ernie 33
DeBusschere, Dave 9, 21,
 21, 34, **34**, 36, **36**
Duncan, Tim.......................**23**
Dukes, Walter...................28, **28**
Dumars, Joe.............17, 22, **22**,
 29, 40, **40**, 43
Eckman, Charley........25, 34, **34**
Edwards, James...................**41**
Groat, Dick........................36
Ham, Darvin........................**10**
Hamilton, Ralph...................**14**
Hamilton, Richard..........15, 18,
 23, 38
Hill, Grant..............14, 23, 35,
 35, 38, **38**, 40, **40**
Howell, Bailey 9
Jackson, Phil.......................26
Jeannette, Buddy...............7, 17
Joe the Brow.......................33
Johnson, Magic....................17
Johnson, Vinnie.....13, 17, 37, **41**

Laimbeer, Bill.................13, 17
Lanier, Bob...............9, 13, 21,
 21, 36, 43
Malone, Karl.......................26
McDermott, Bobby........7, **7**, 16,
 16, 17, 20, 40, 43
Meineke, Don......................40
Mendenhall, Murray 30
Mikan, George 30, **31**
Milicic, Darko.....................**43**
National Basketball
League (NBL) 7
O'Neal, Shaquille........18, 26, 27
Palace of Auburn
Hills...............**12**, 13, 27, 33
Payton, Gary 26
Pelkington, Jake 17
Pontiac Silverdome...............36
Prince, Tayshaun 18
Rodman, Dennis....17, 22, 40, 43
Sadowski, Ed..................17, **17**
Salley, John **41**
Scott, Ray 40
Thomas, Isiah 9, **9**, 13,
 17, 22, 37, 37, 39, **39**, 40, 43
Wallace, Ben..................10, 18,
 23, **23**, 27, **27**,
 ....37, **37**, 39, 40
Wallace, Rasheed........18, 23, **23**
World Professional Basketball
Tournament.............7, 16, 41
Yardley, George........**8**, 9, 20, **20**,
 29, **29**, 38, 43
Zollner, Fred 6, **6**, 7,
 9, 16, 25, 29
Zollner Machine Works...........7

The Team

MARK STEWART has written more than 20 books on basketball, and over 100 sports books for kids. He grew up in New York City during the 1960s rooting for the Knicks and Nets, and now takes his two daughters, Mariah and Rachel, to watch them play. Mark comes from a family of writers. His grandfather was Sunday Editor of *The New York Times* and his mother was Articles Editor of *The Ladies Home Journal* and *McCall's*. Mark has profiled hundreds of athletes over the last 20 years. He has also written several books about his native New York, and New Jersey, his home today. Mark is a graduate of Duke University, with a degree in history. He lives with his daughters and wife, Sarah, overlooking Sandy Hook, NJ.

MATT ZEYSING is the resident historian at the Basketball Hall of Fame in Springfield, Massachusetts. His research interests include the origins of the game of basketball, the development of professional basketball in the first half of the twentieth century, and the culture and meaning of basketball in American society.